MEDITATIVE MANDALAS BY SIMI

SIMI RAGHAVAN

This book belongs to

_____

_____

ISBN-13: 978-1542355070
ISBN-10: 1542355079

Other books by Artist Simi Raghavan:

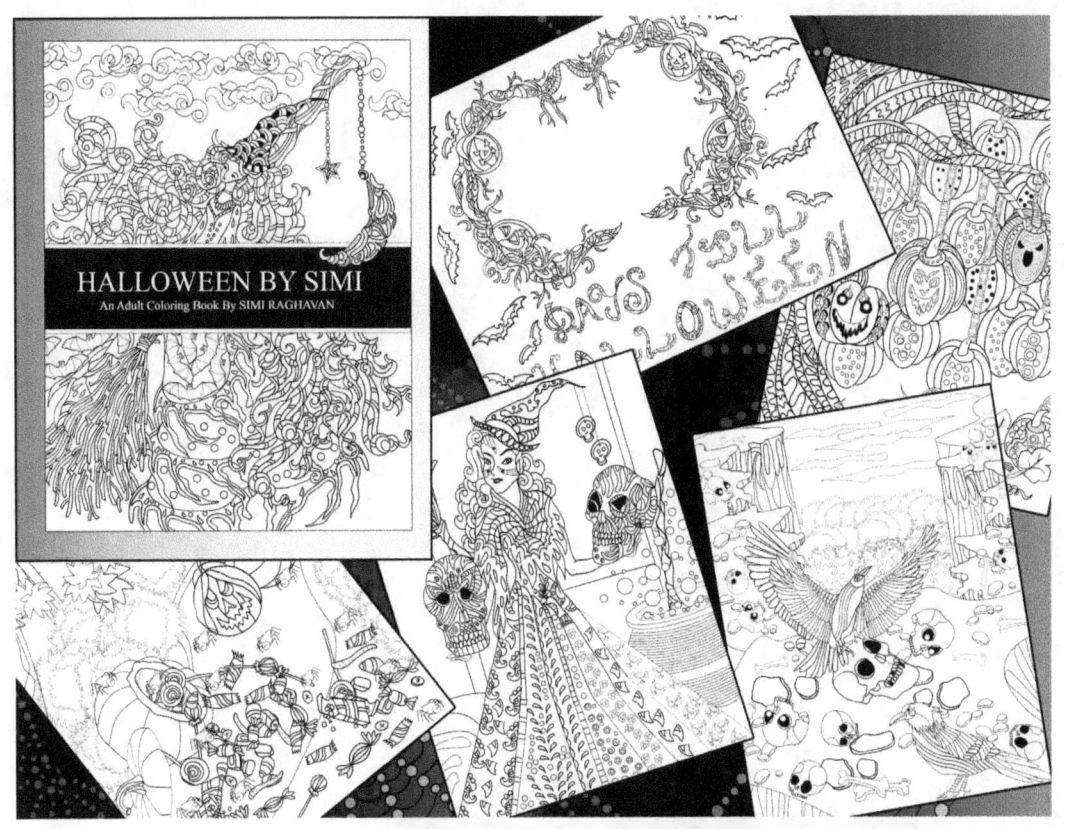

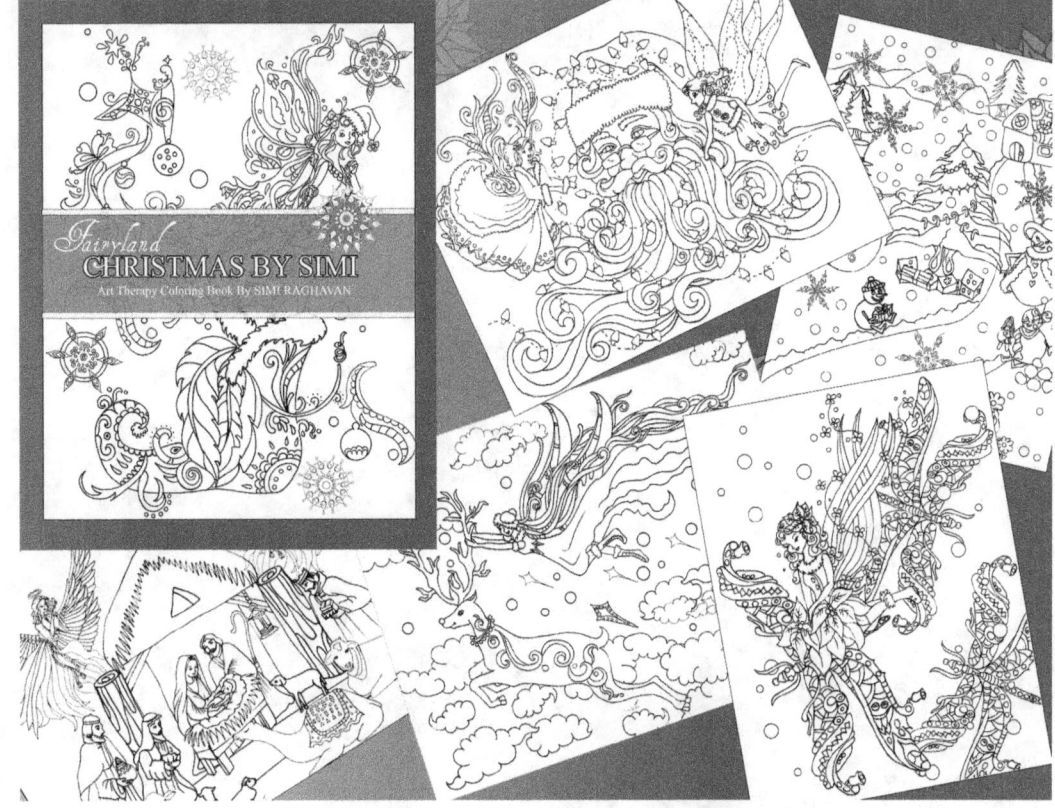

About the Artist.

Simi lives in the exotic land of Kerala, in India. Her artwork flourishes amidst the gorgeous backwaters, the never ending greenery, aroma of chai & spices, mantras & chants from the temples. Meditation and Yoga are common practice here and everything around her inspires her to create new pieces of amazing art. Have fun coloring, leave a review on amazon & don't forget to post your colored pages on her Facebook group.

www.simiraghavan.com
www.amazon.com/author/simiraghavan
www.facebook.com/simiraghavanart
www.facebook.com/groups/simiraghavan
simiraghavanart@gmail.com

"Meditative Mandalas focuses on the calming meditative effect achieved while coloring in repetitive patterns in the circular mandala form. This Art Therapy coloring book is aimed to de-stress & provide inner peace. A must in today's chaotic world. I hope you enjoy coloring in and don't forget to share your colored pieces with me."
-Simi.

PDF copy is available here: https://gum.co/meditativemandalasbysimi

Contents

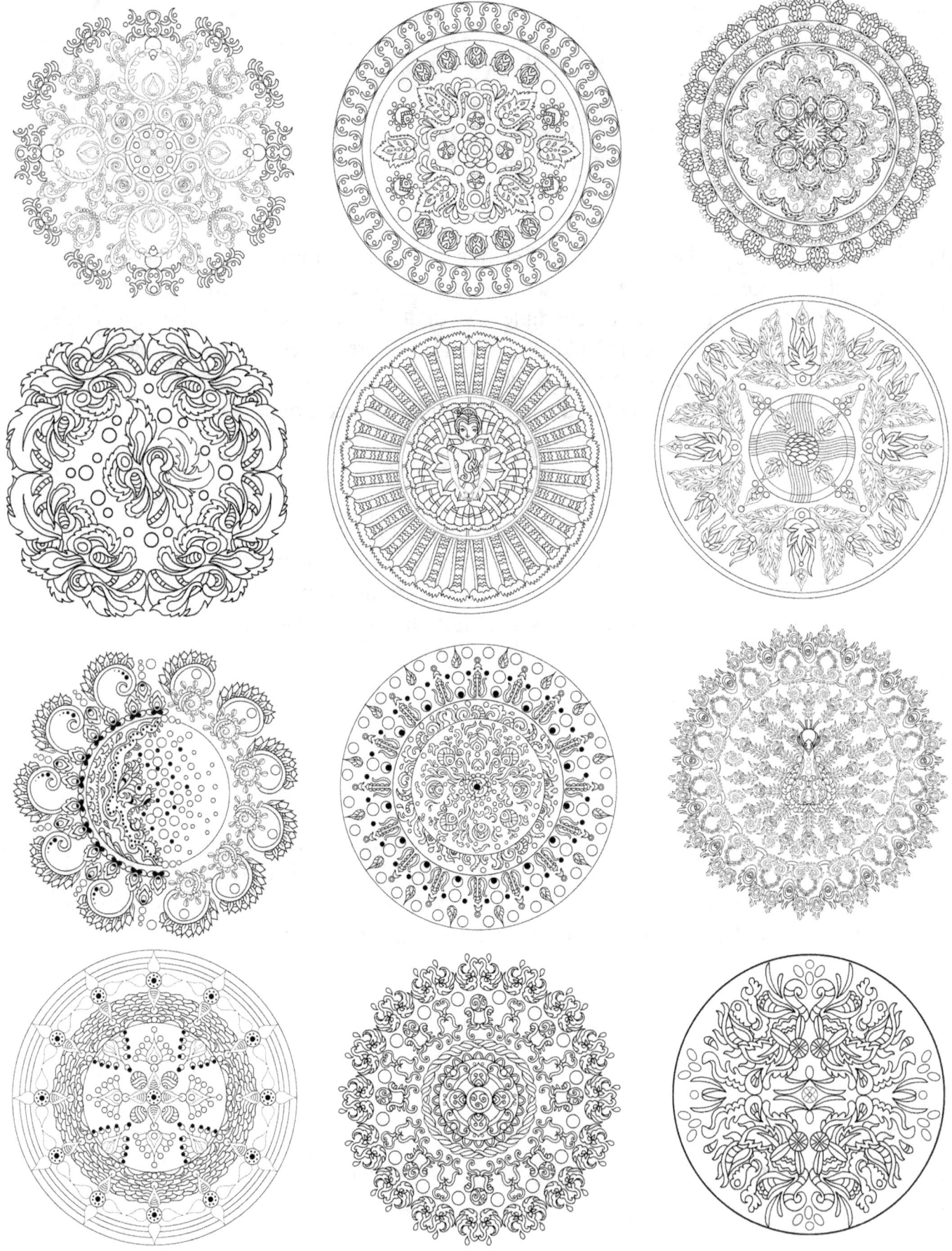

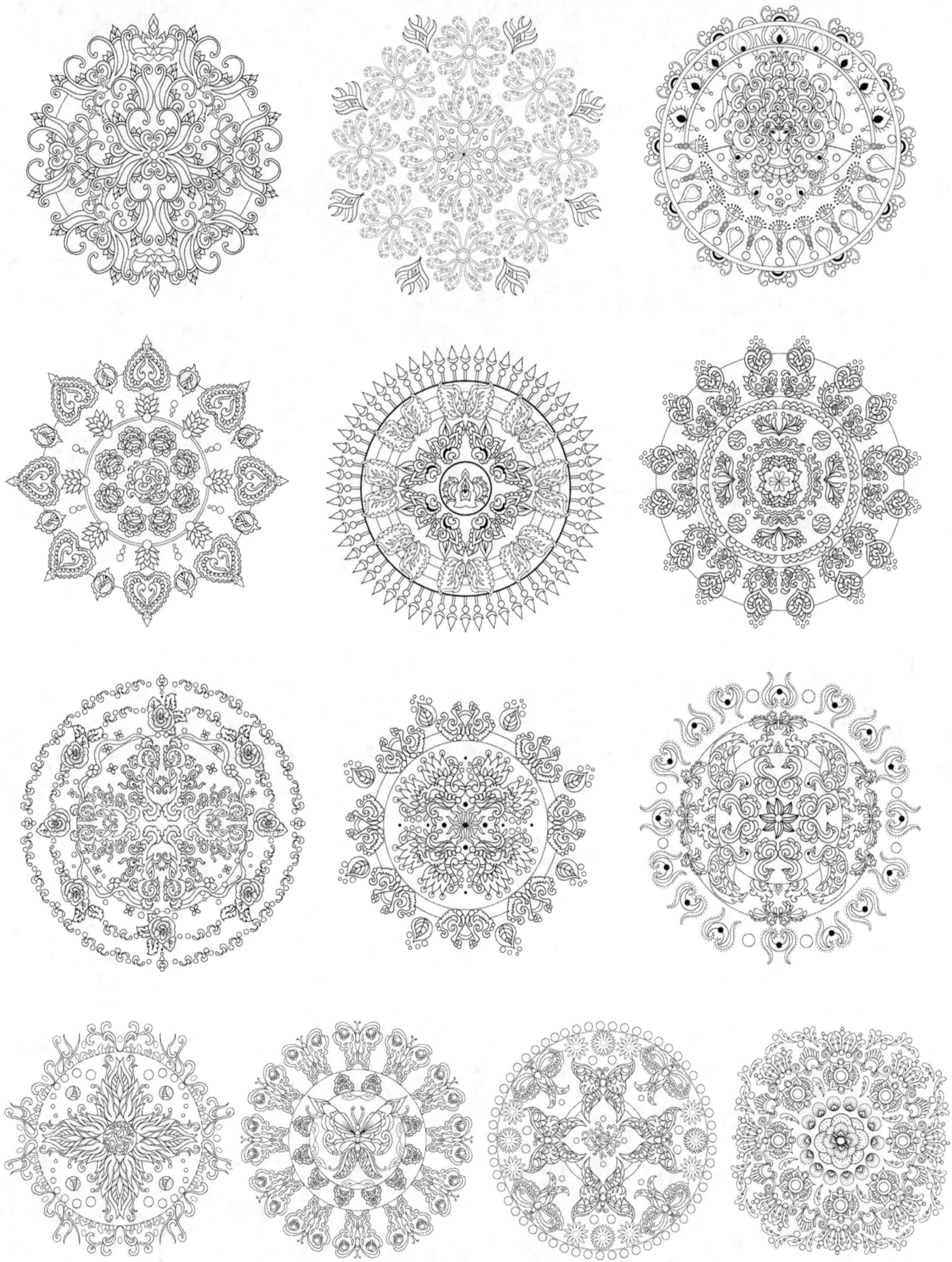

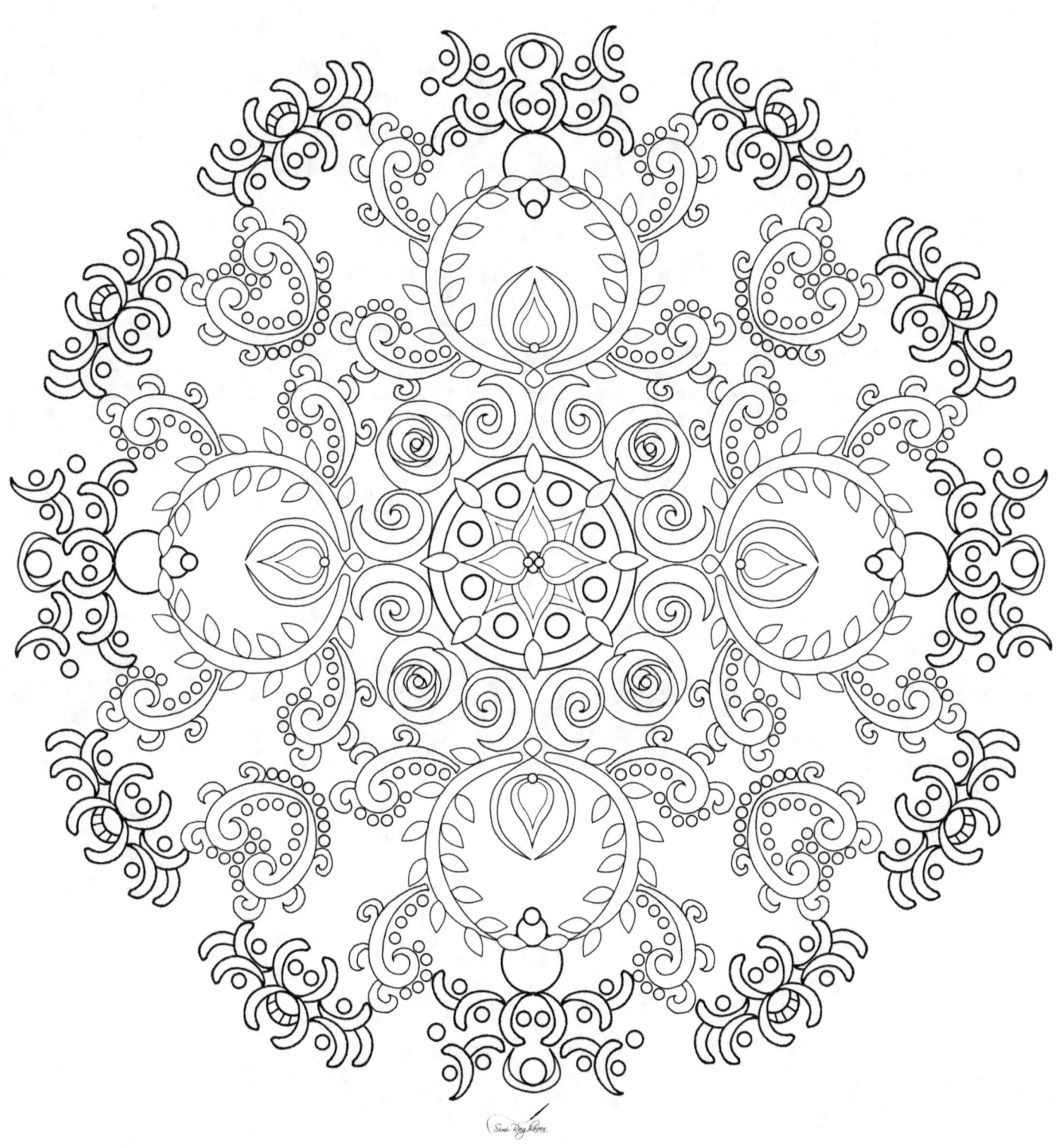

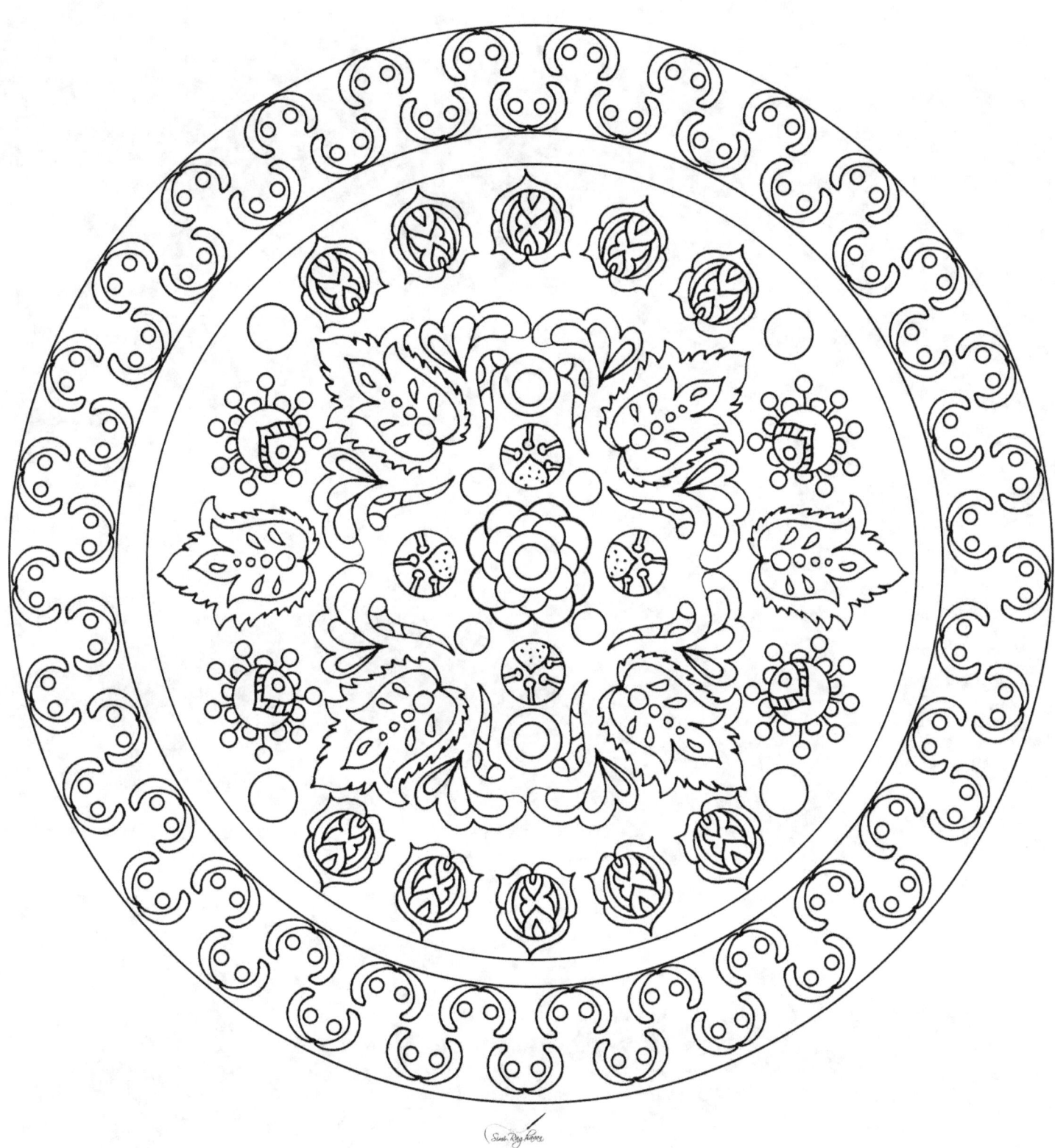

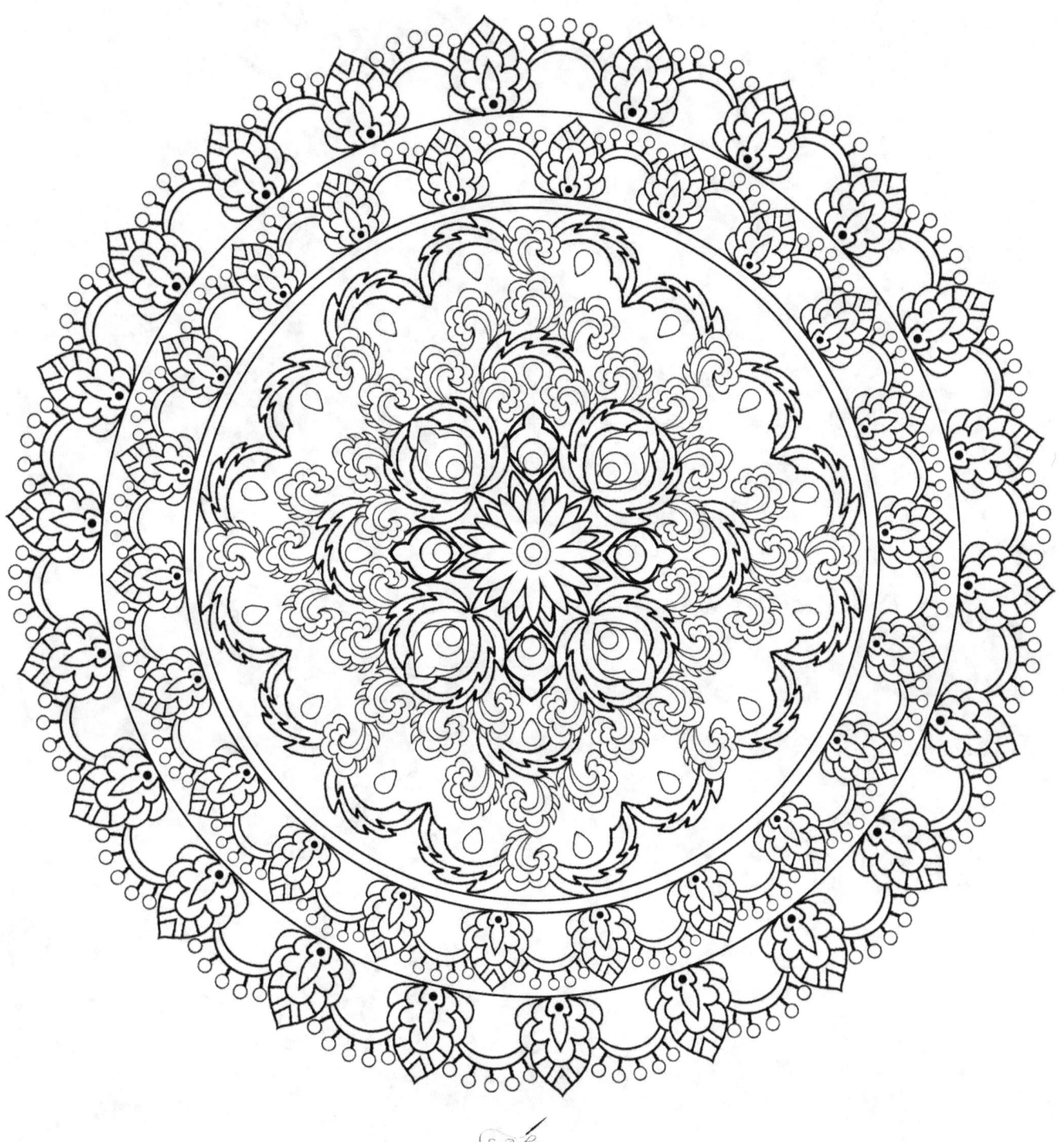

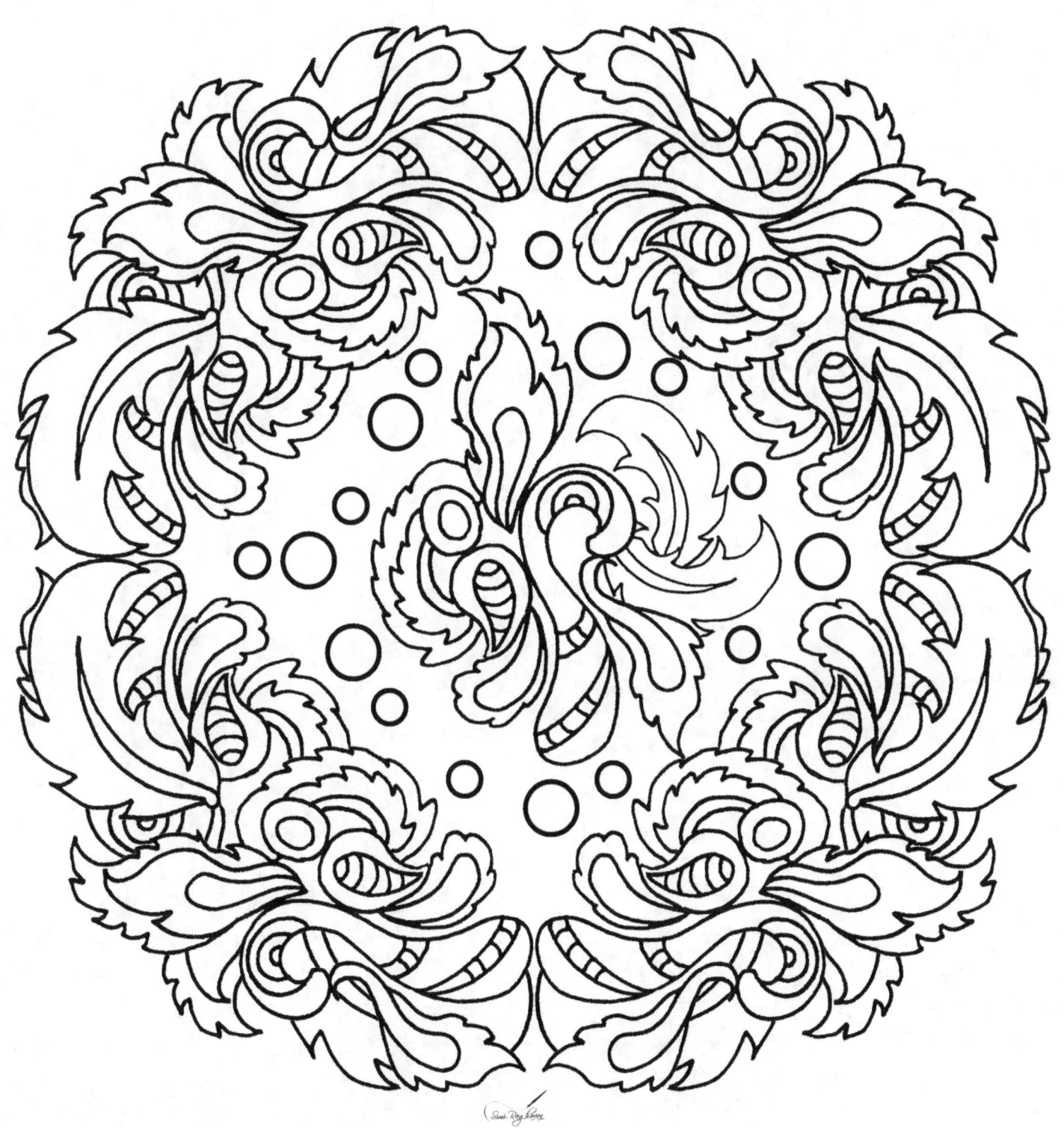

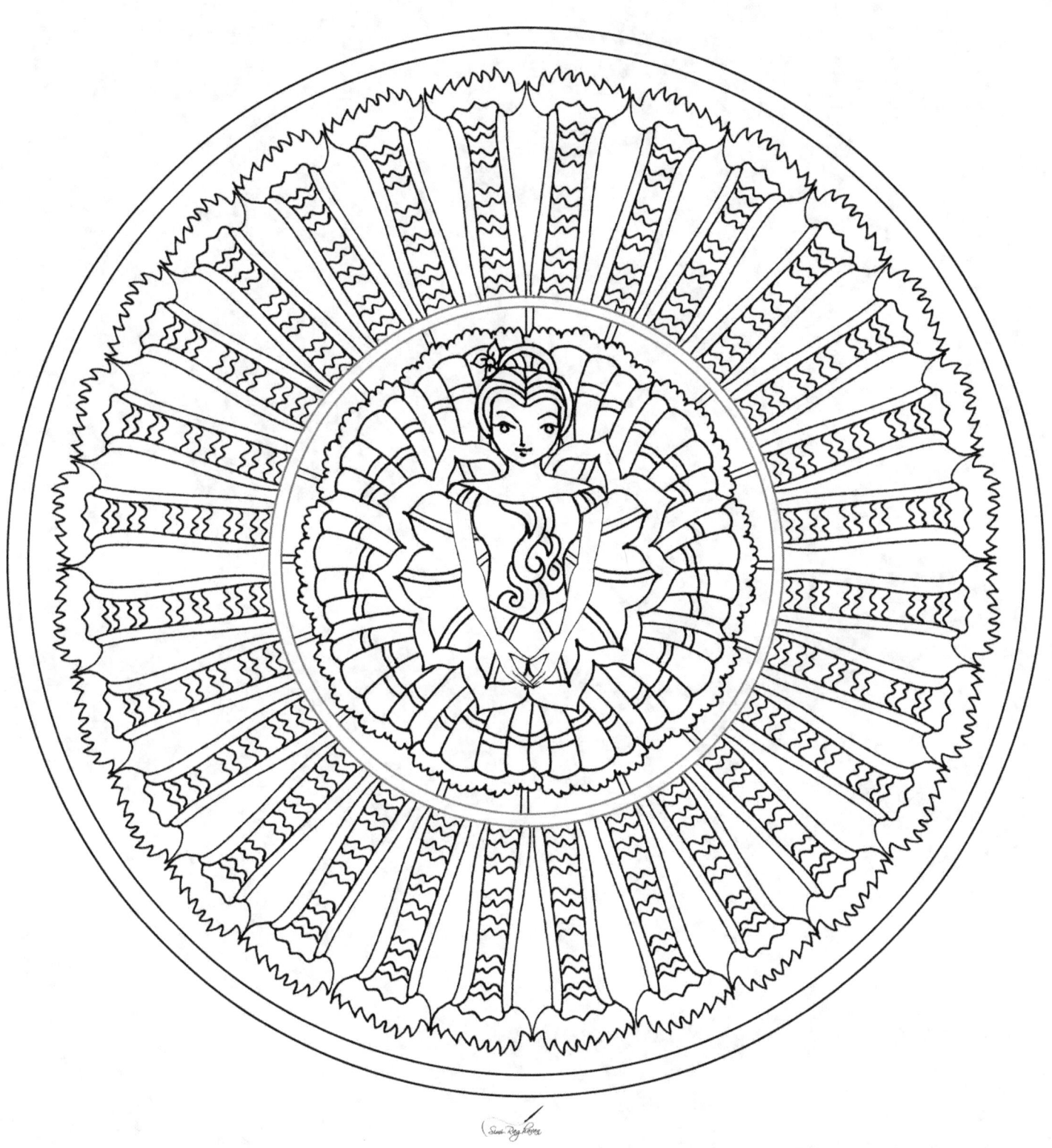

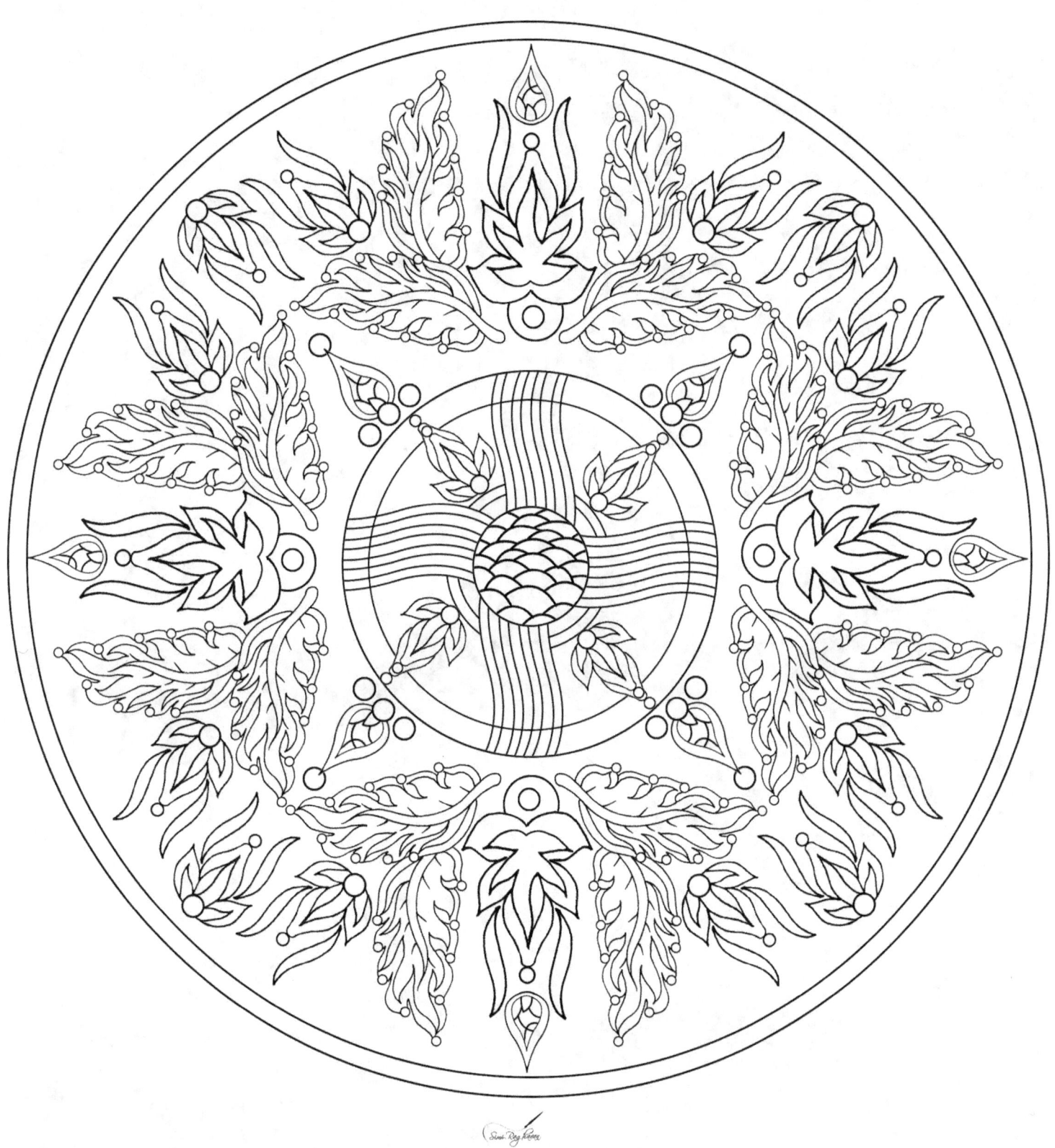

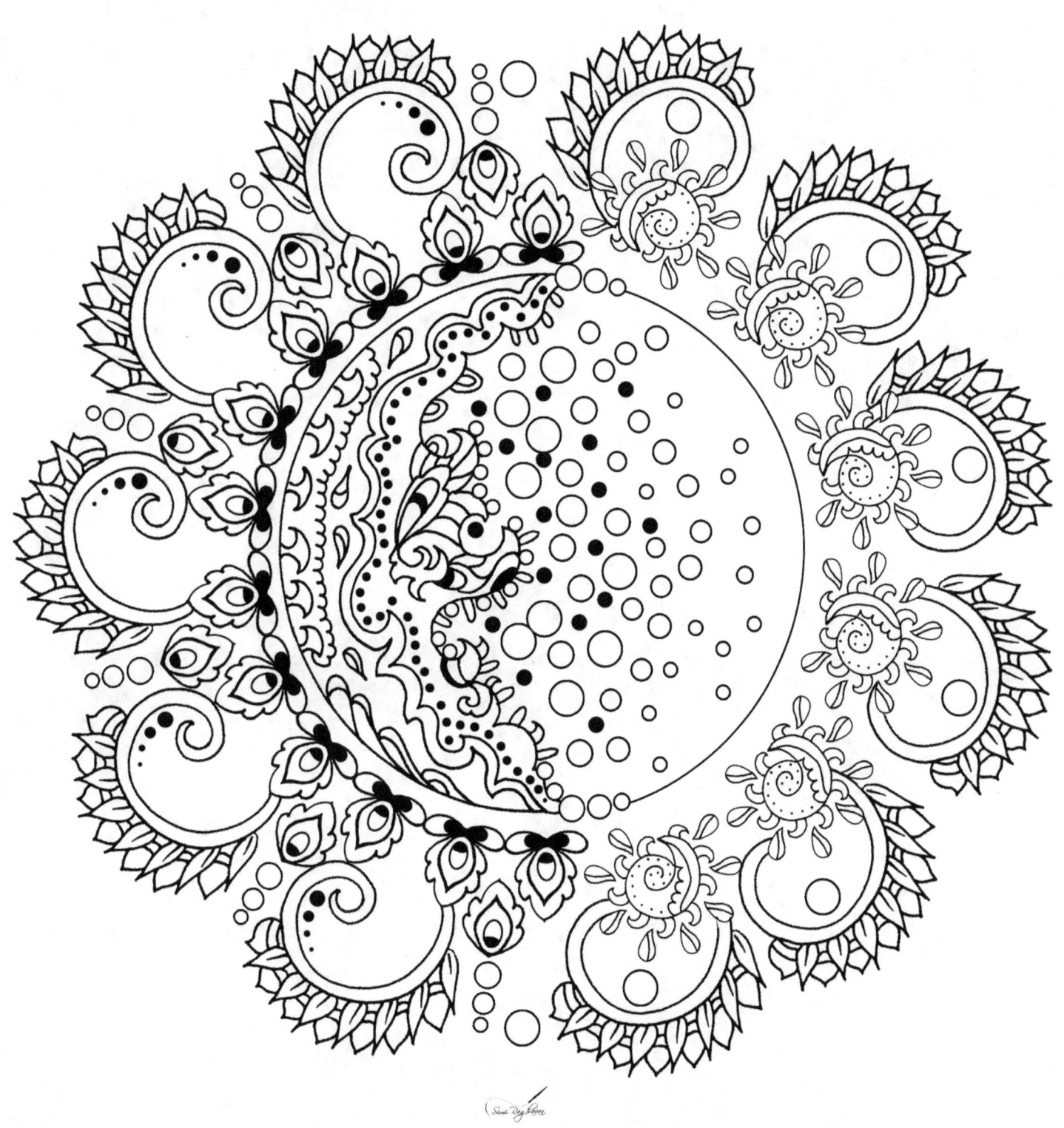

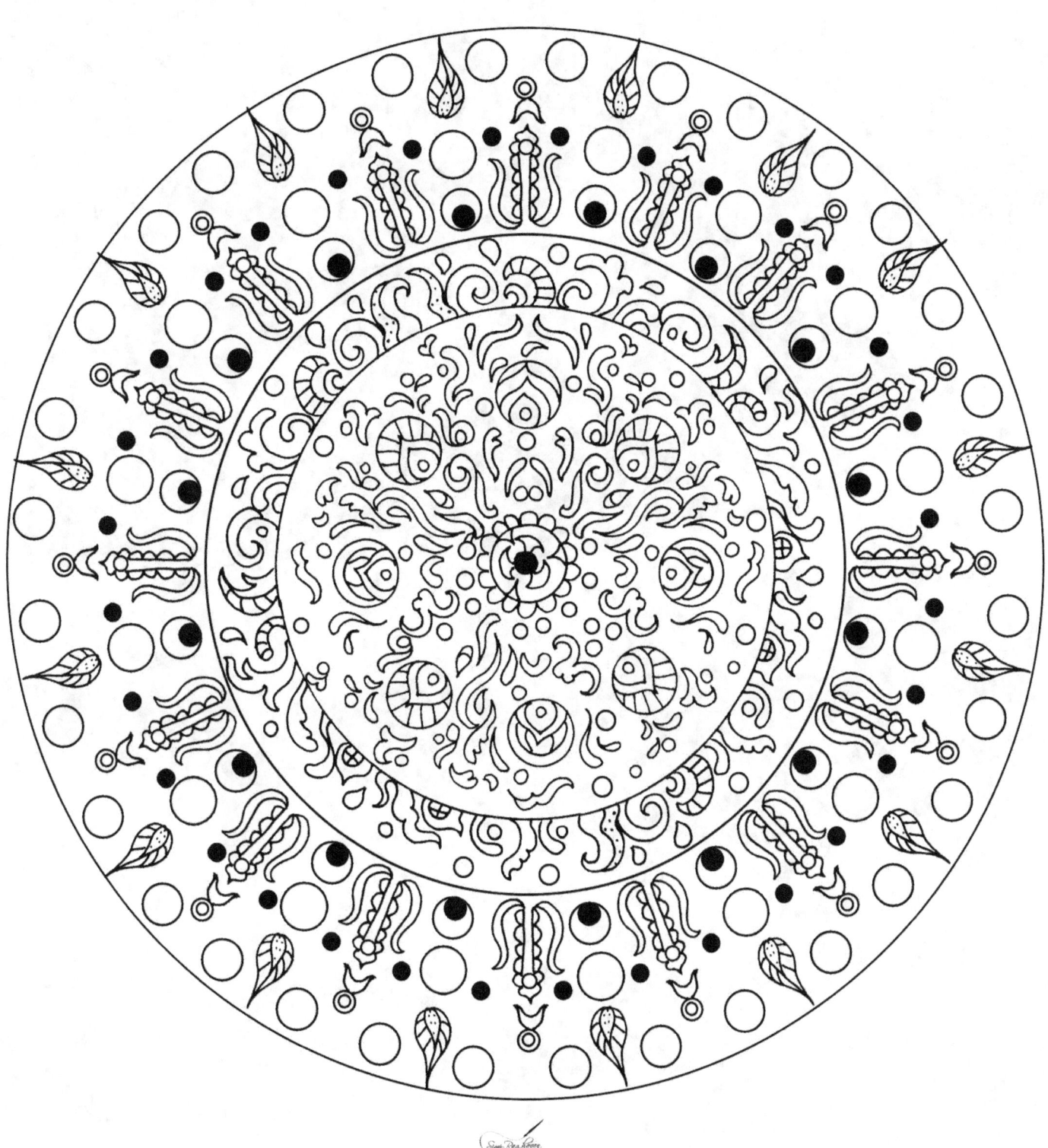

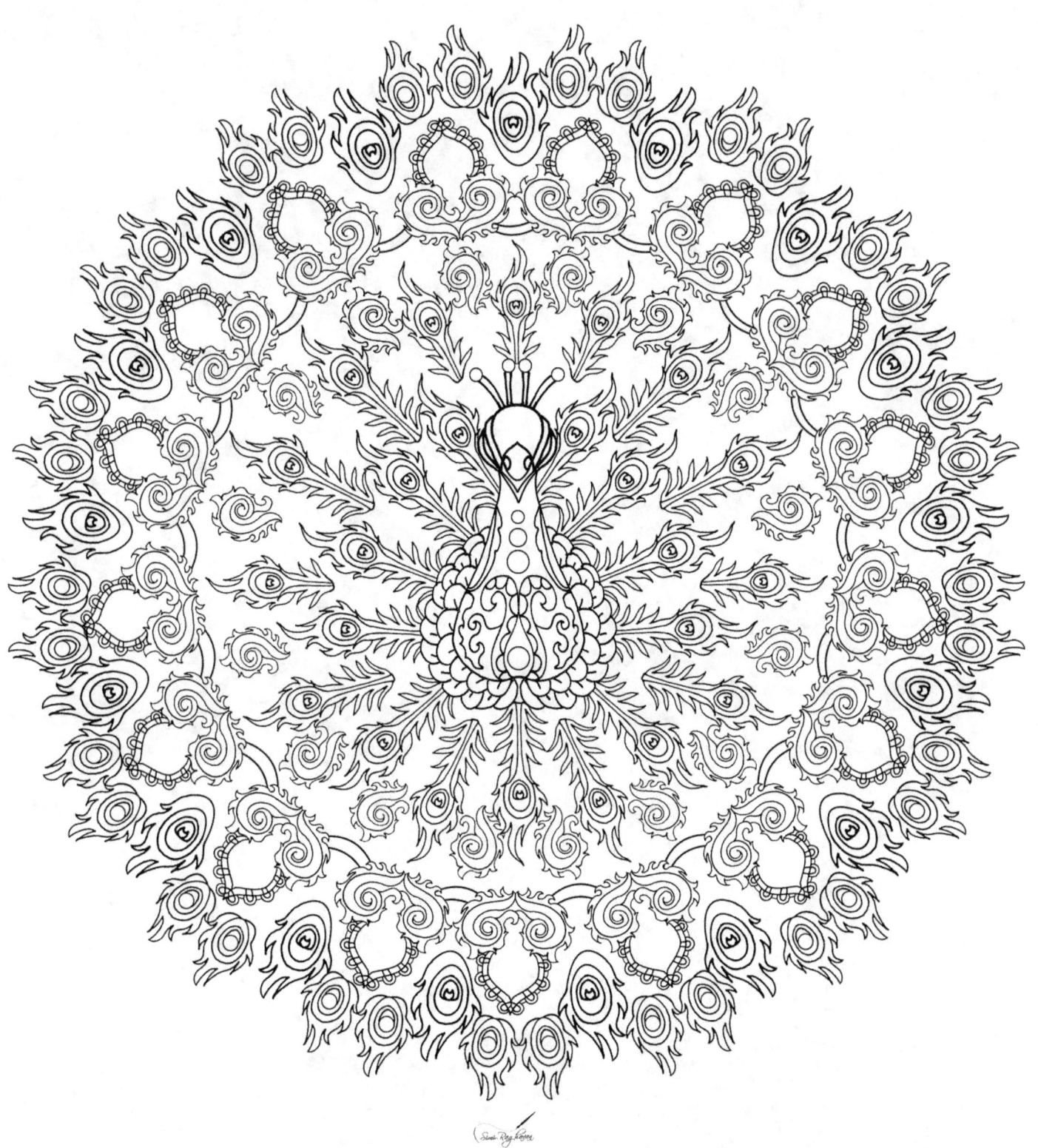

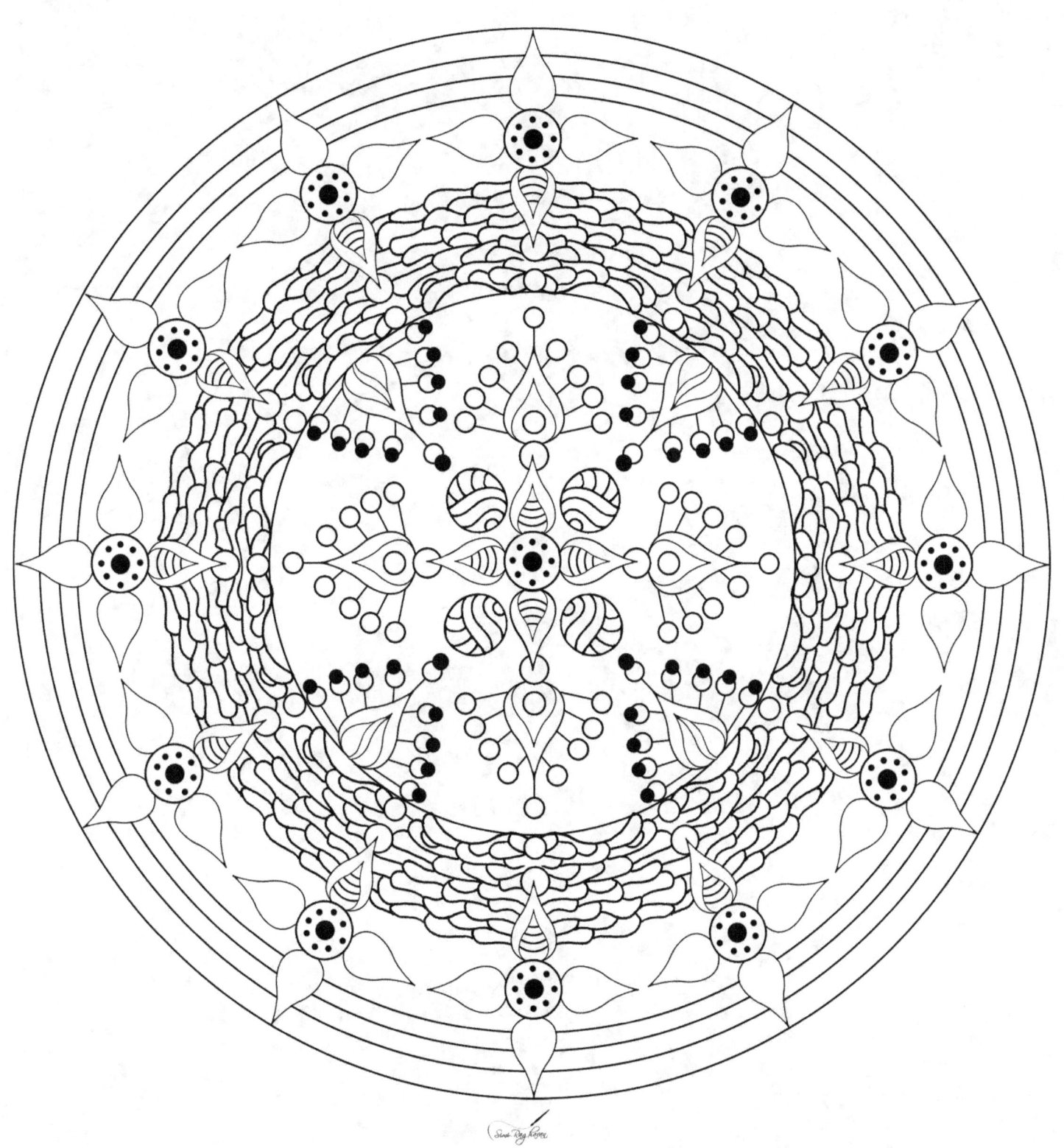

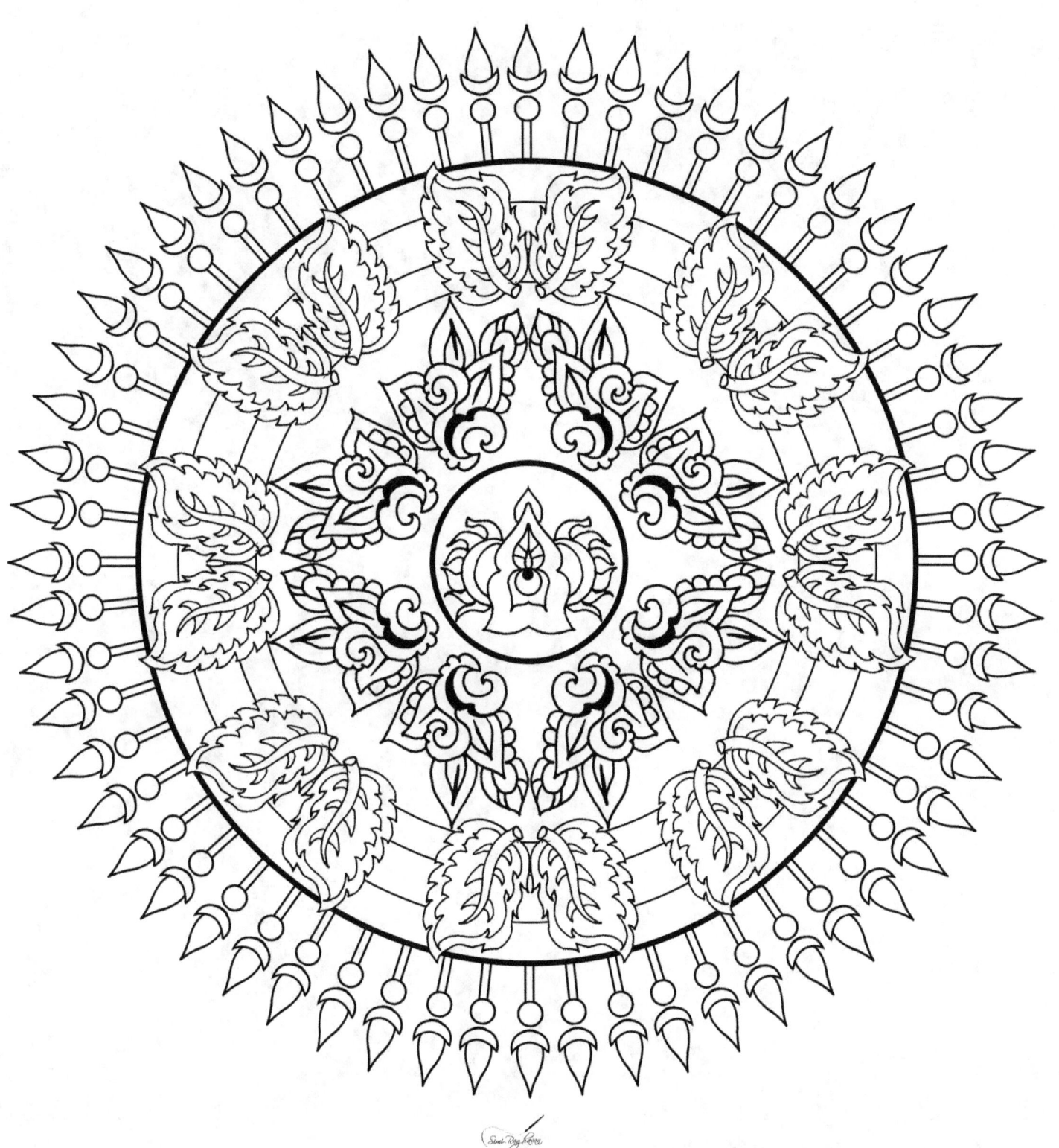

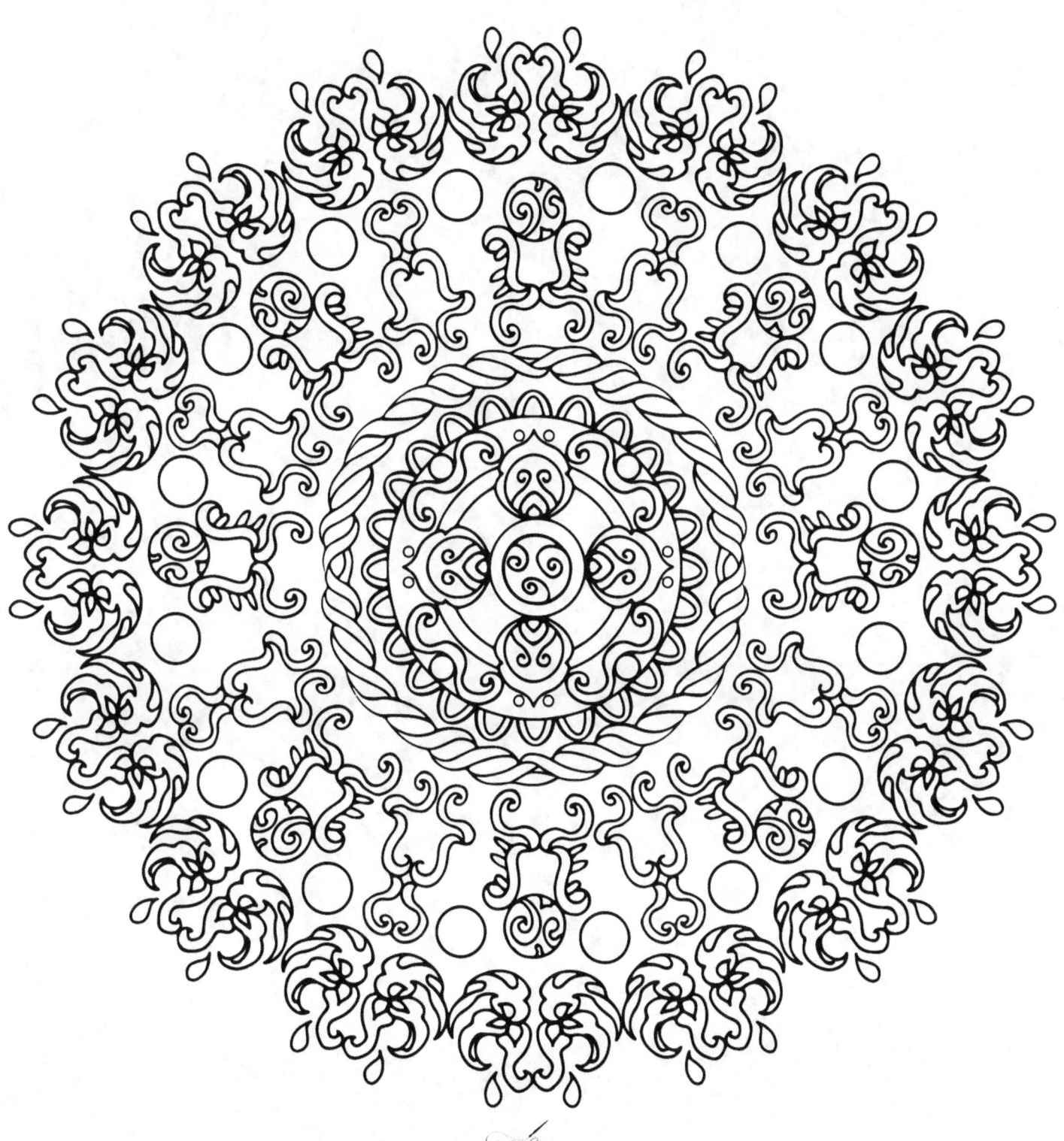

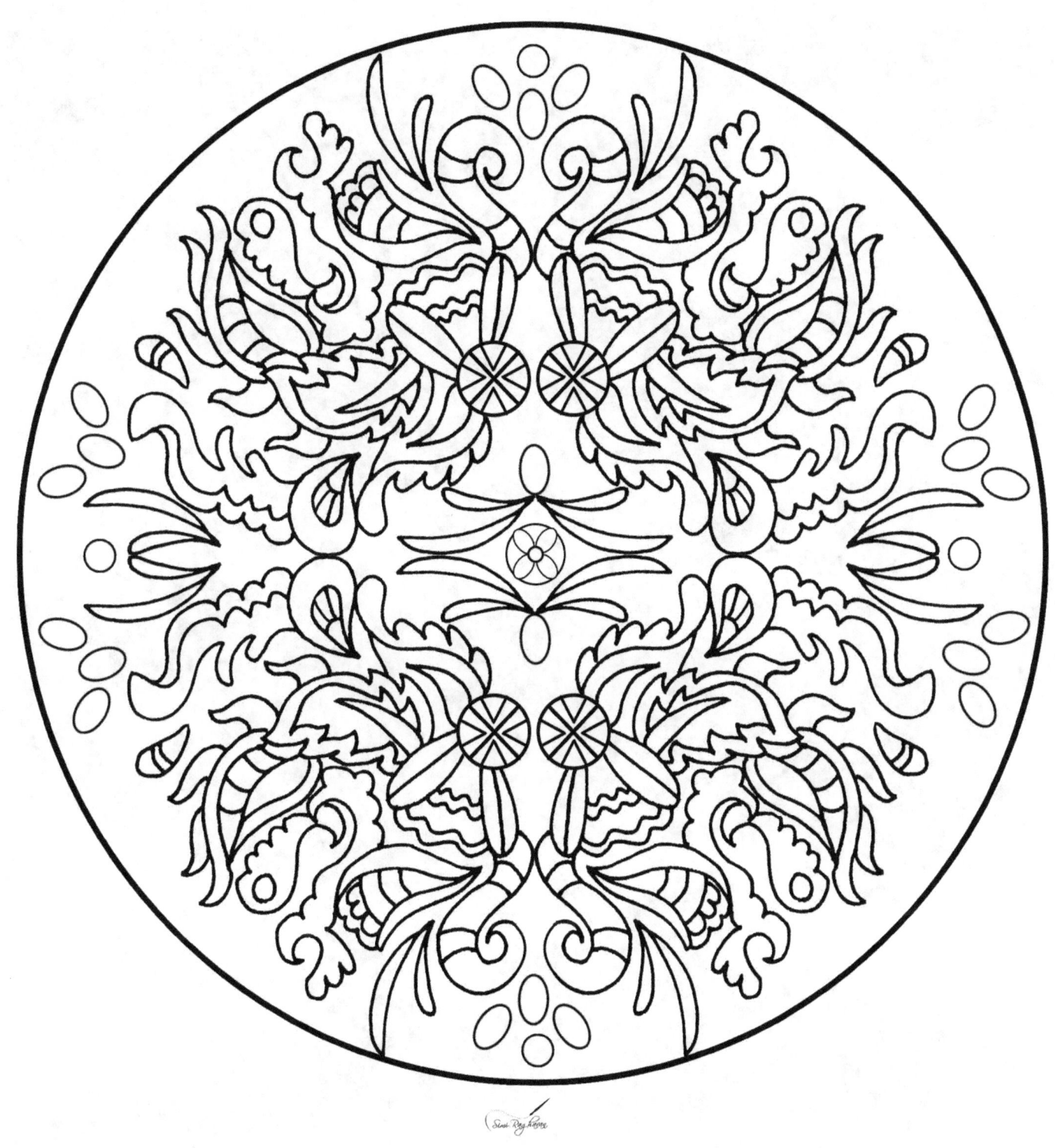

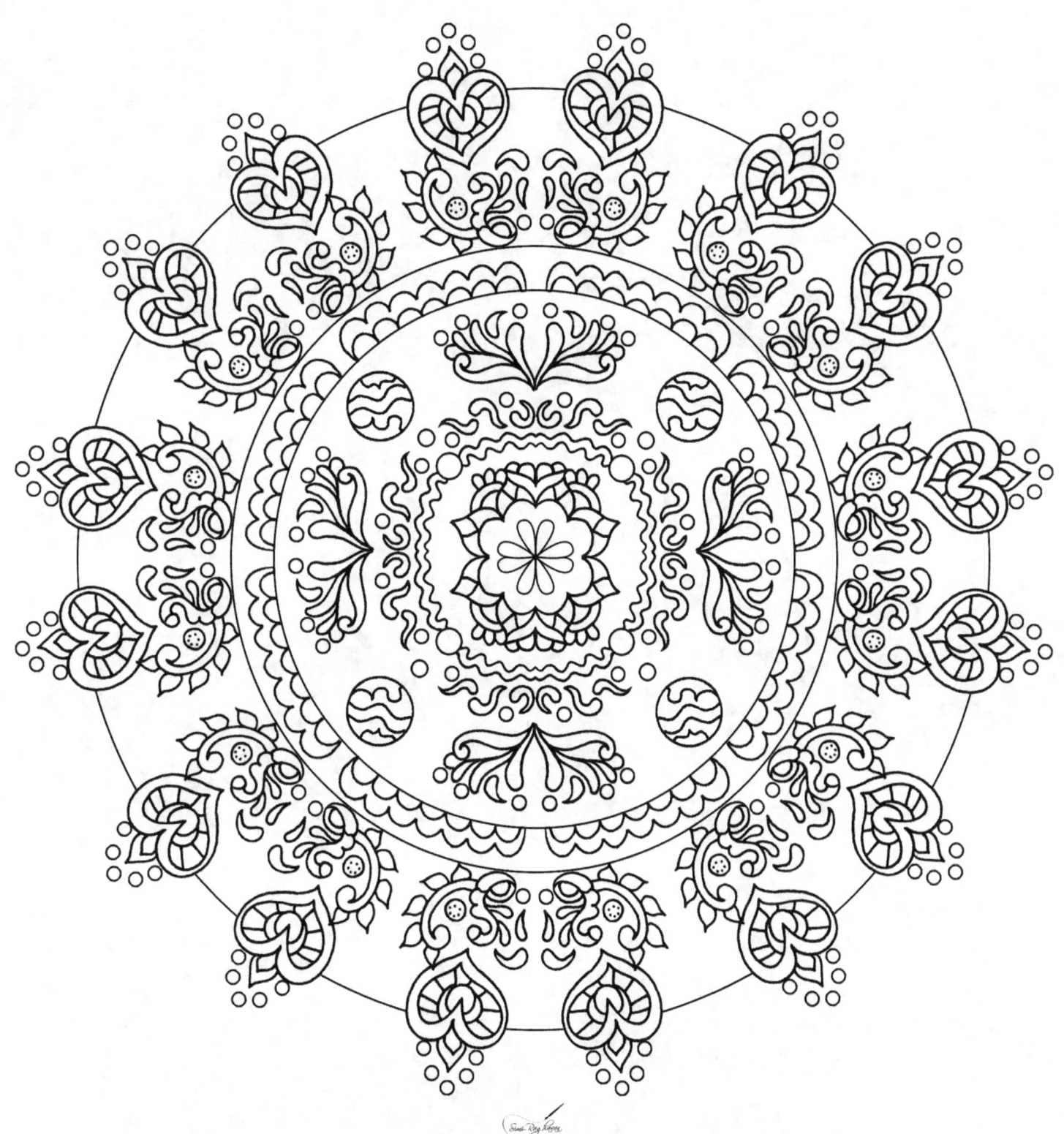

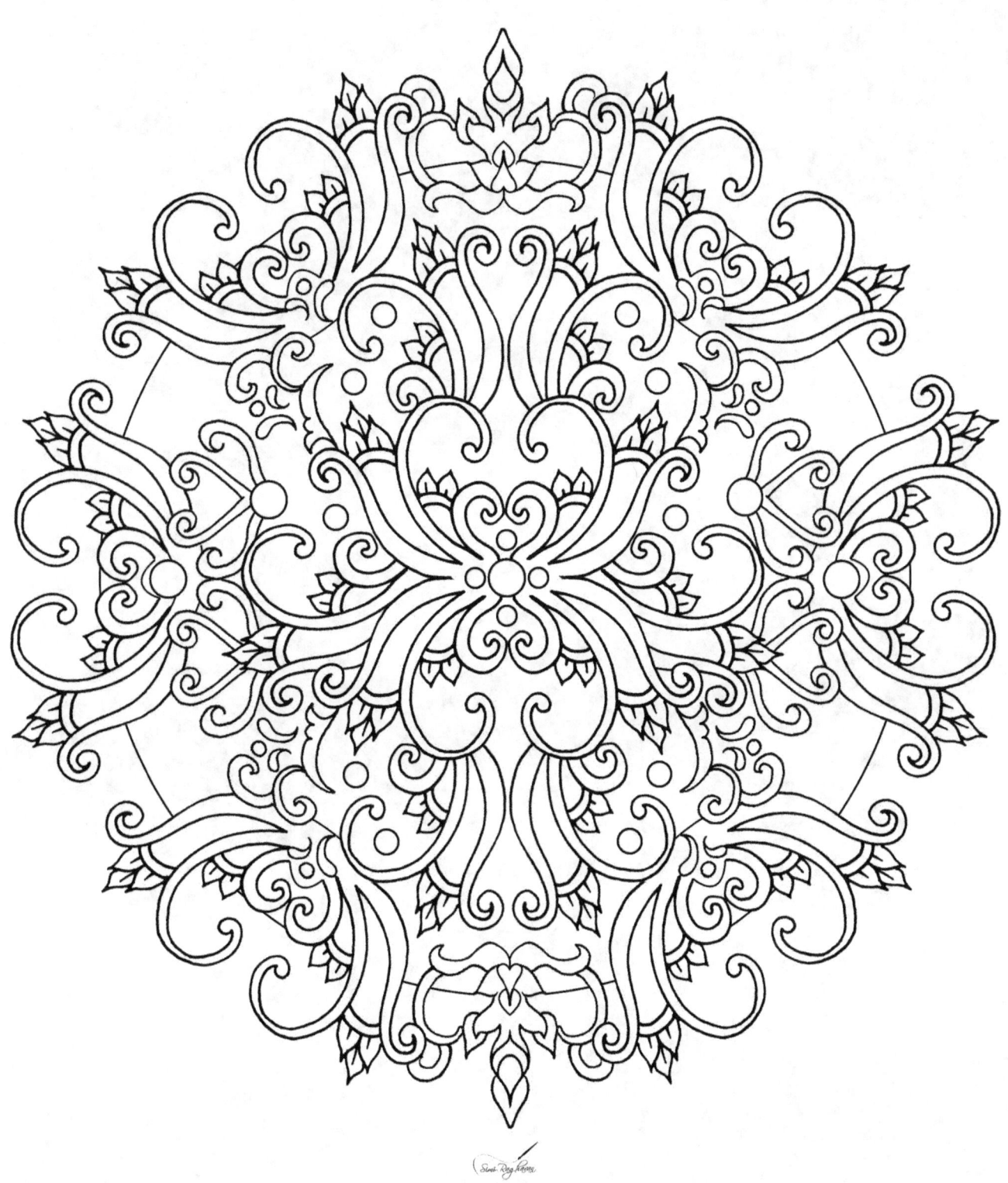

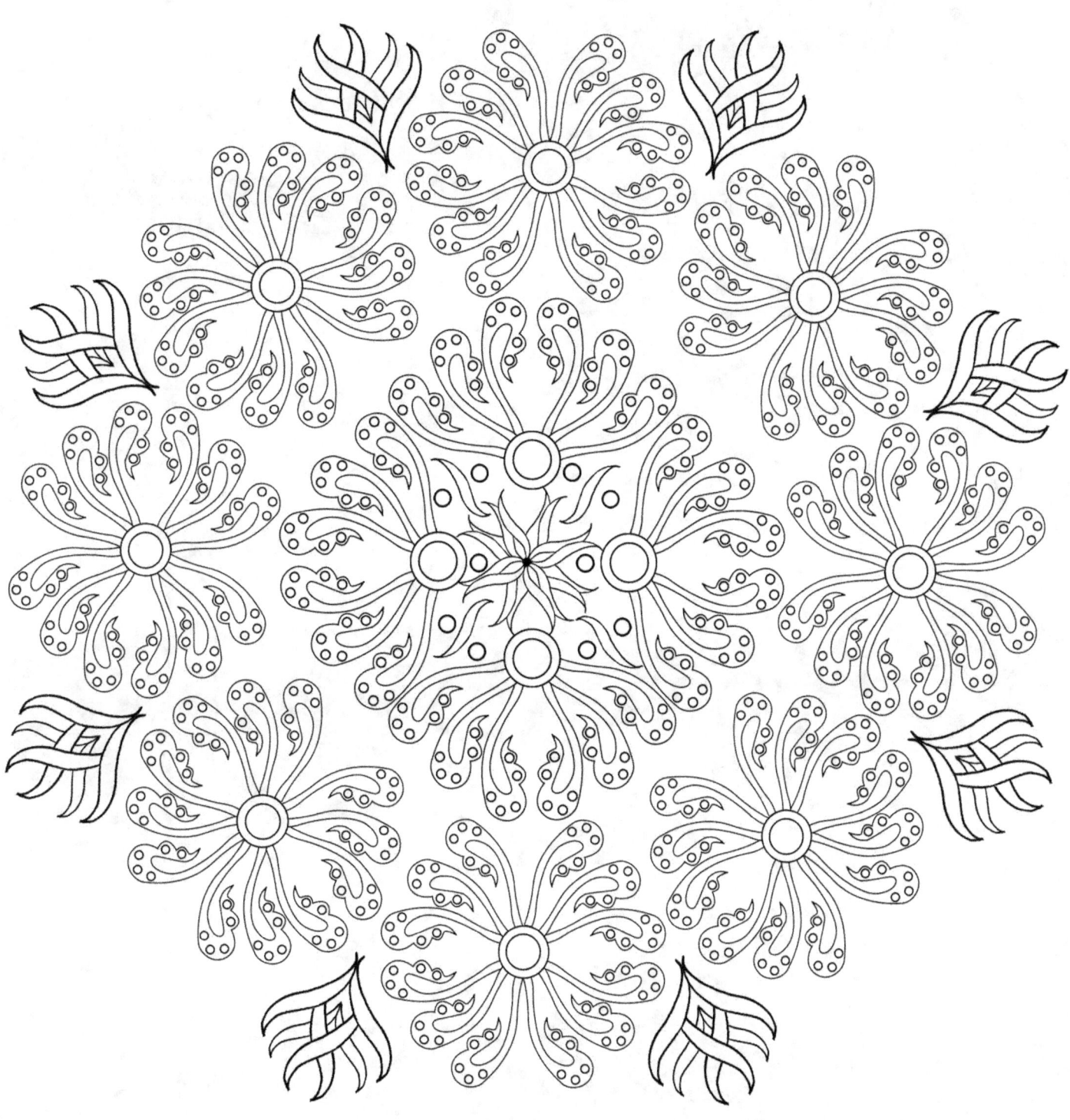

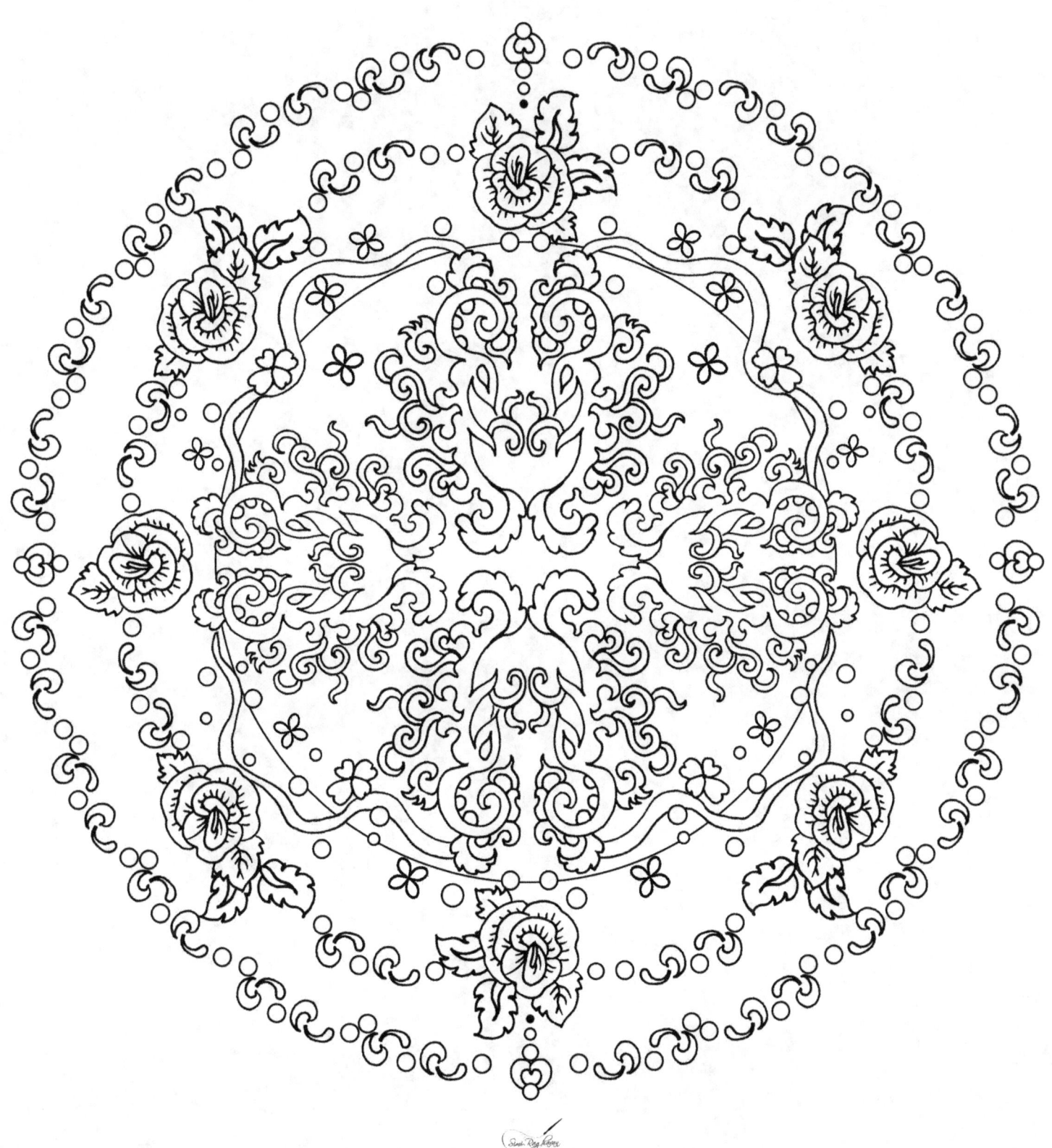

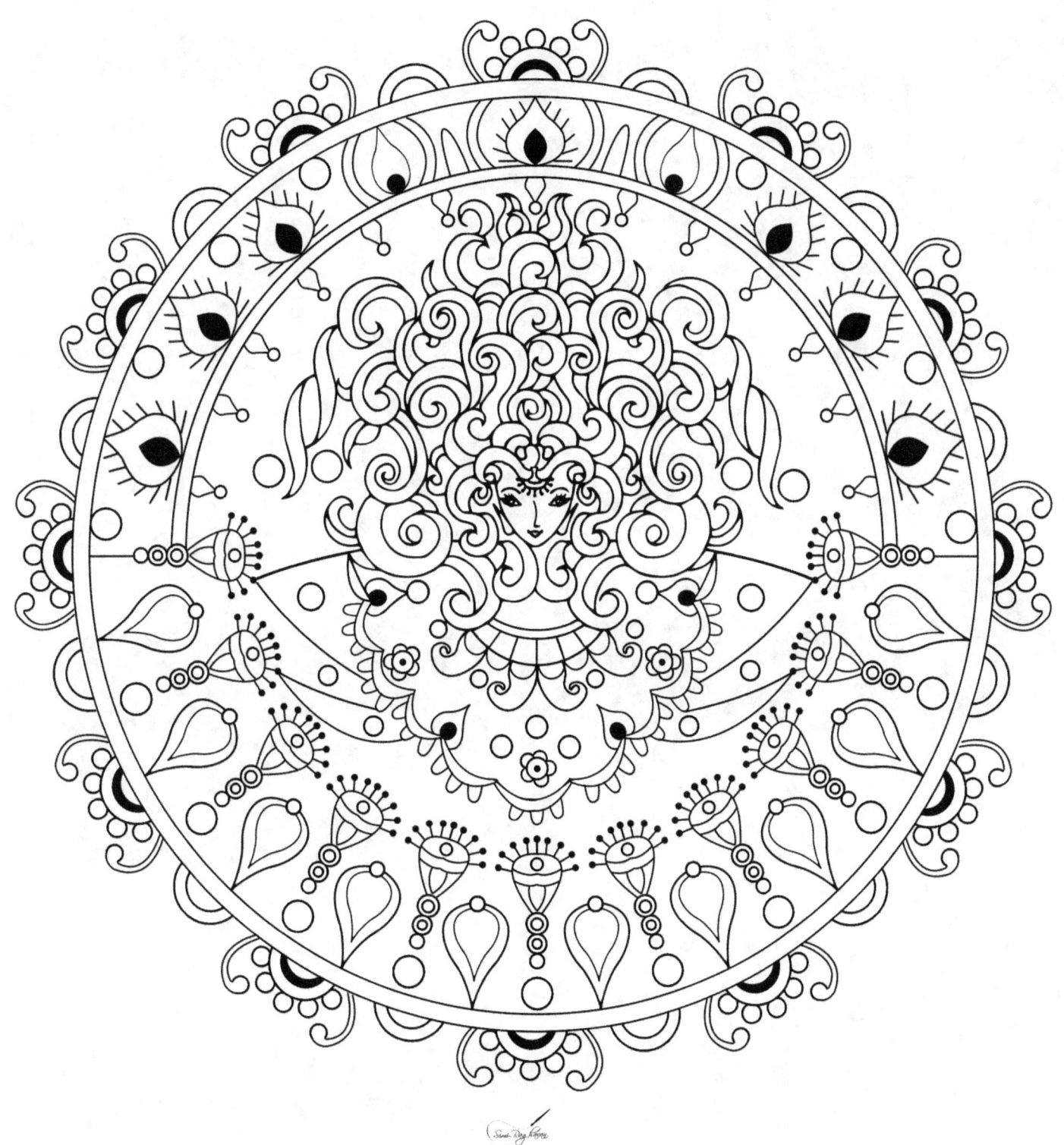

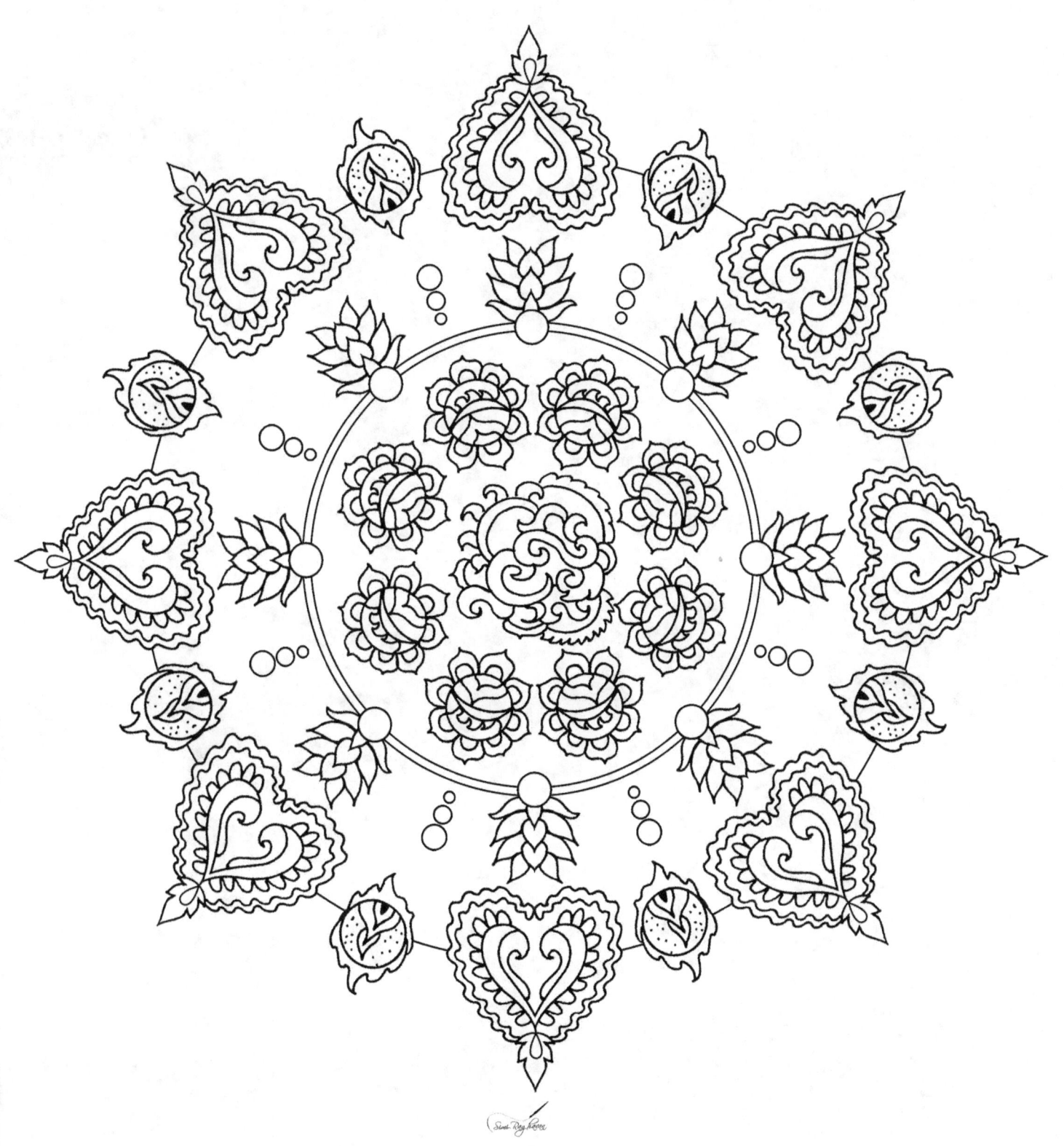

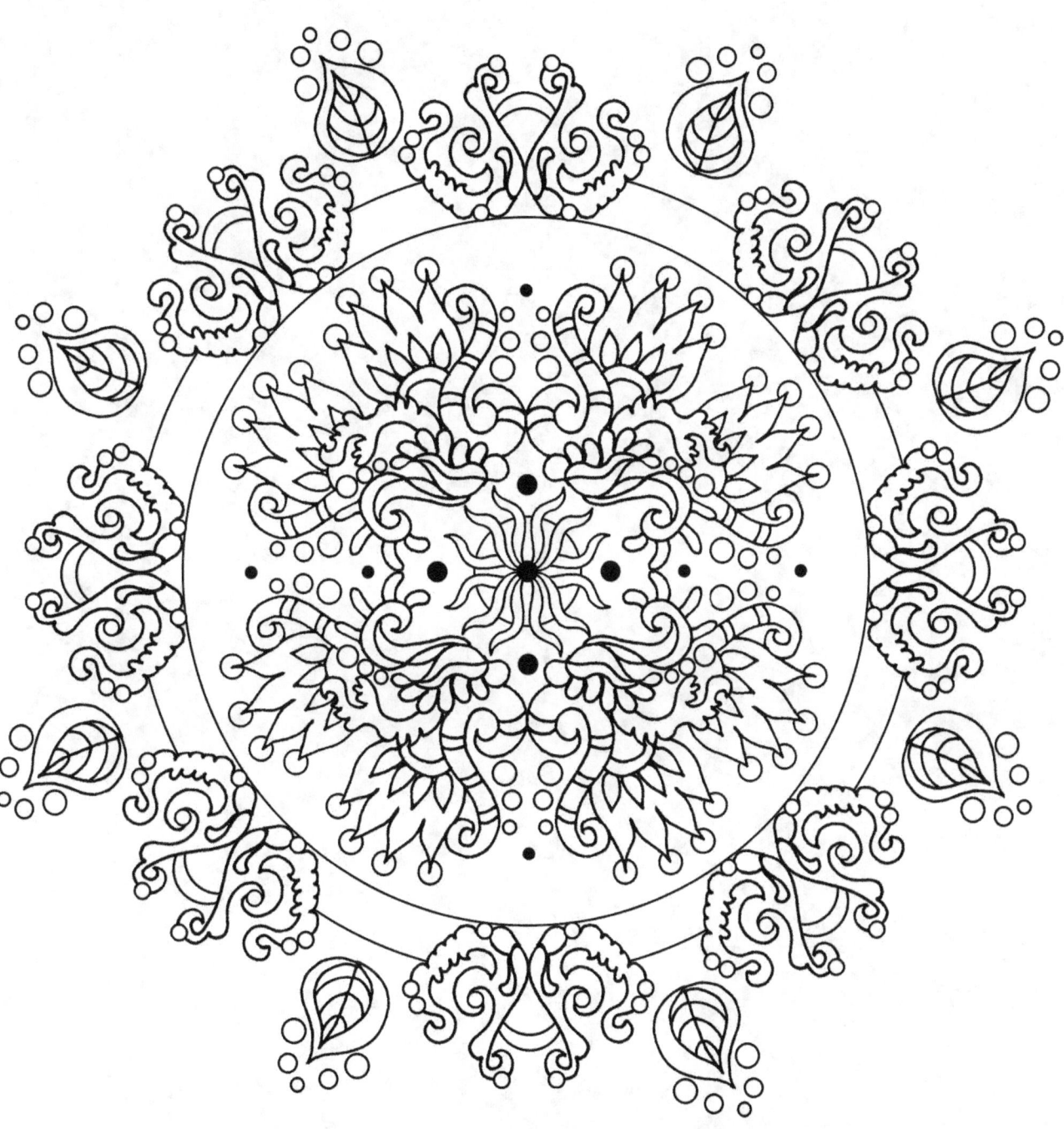

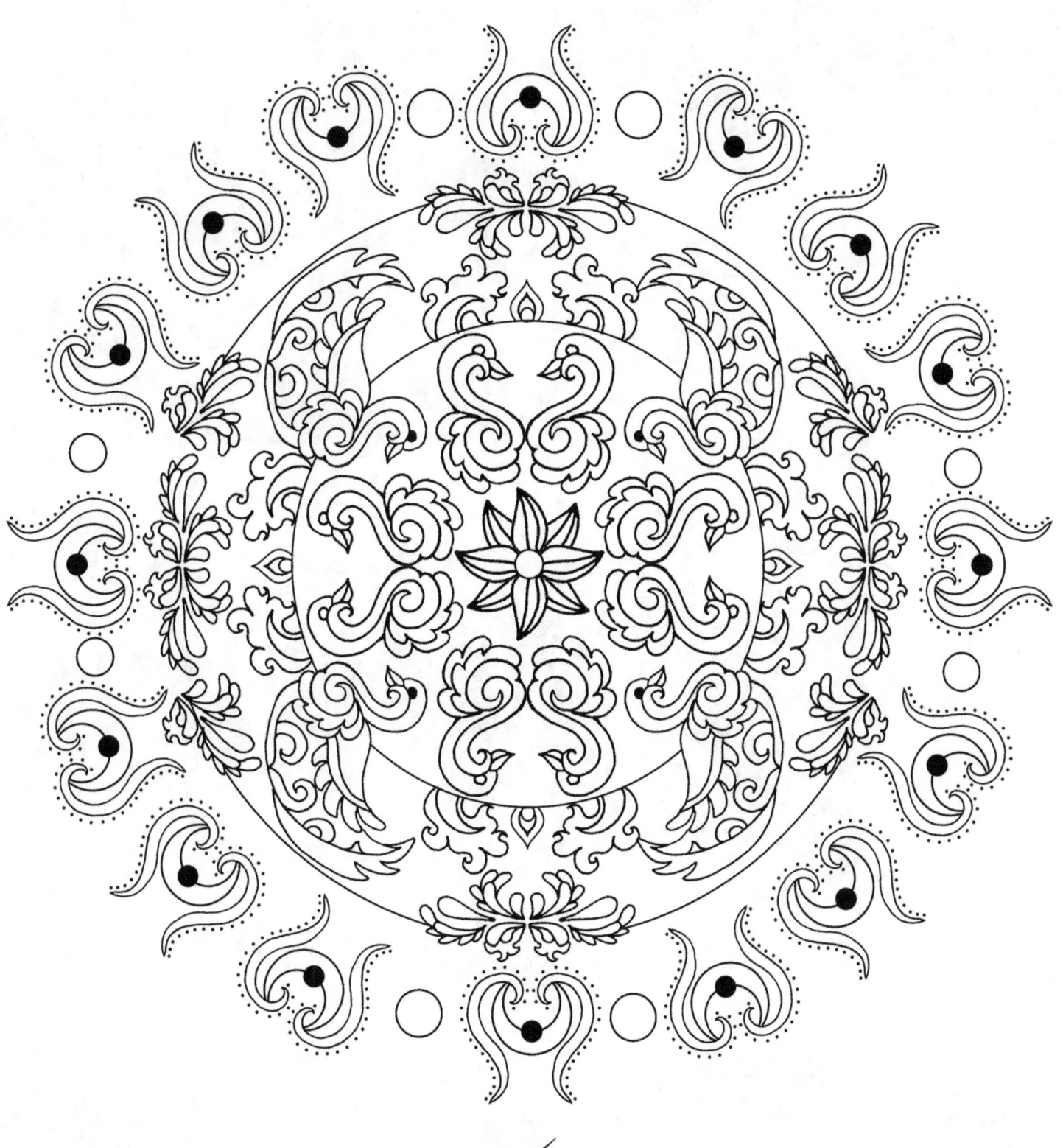

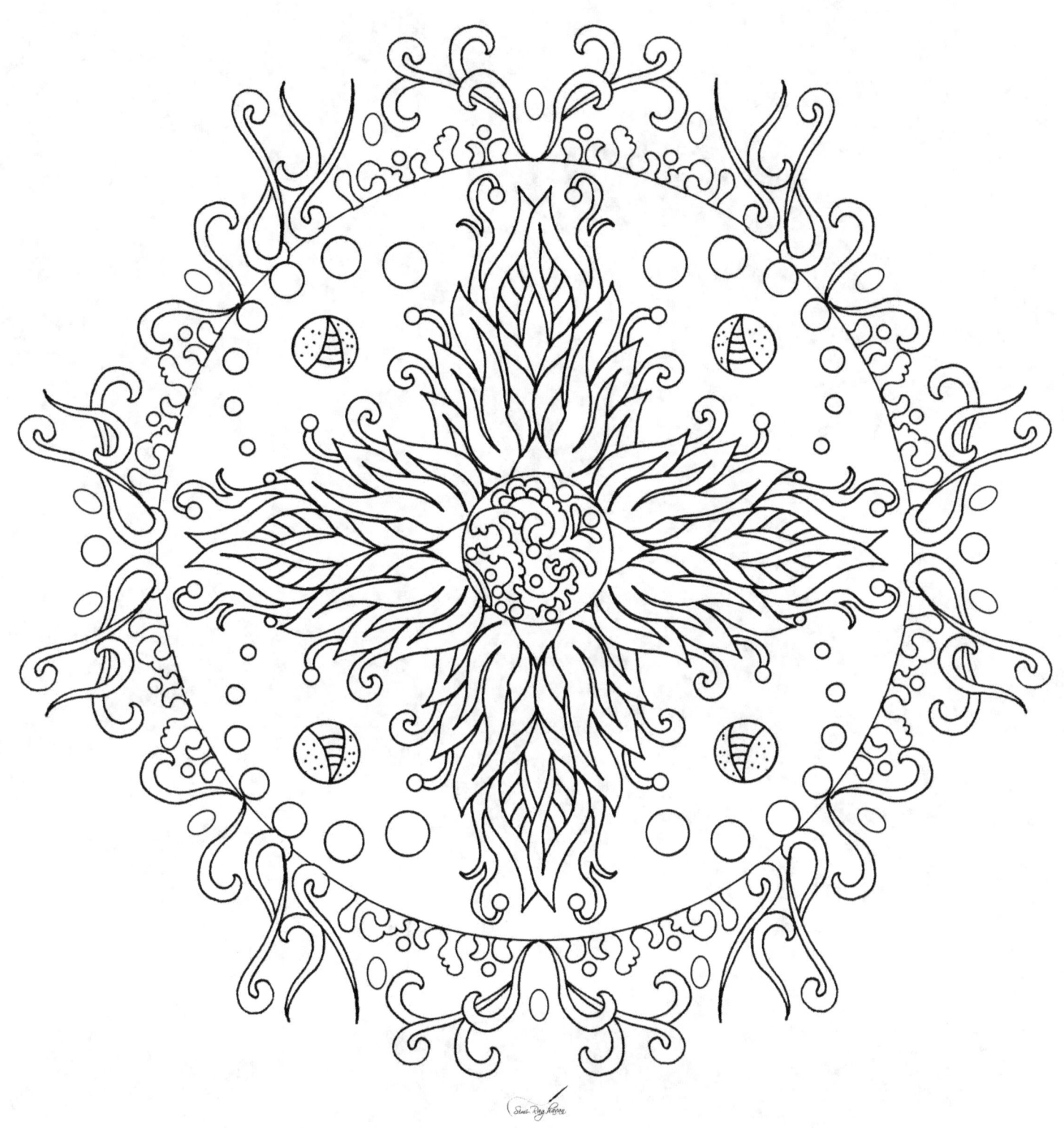

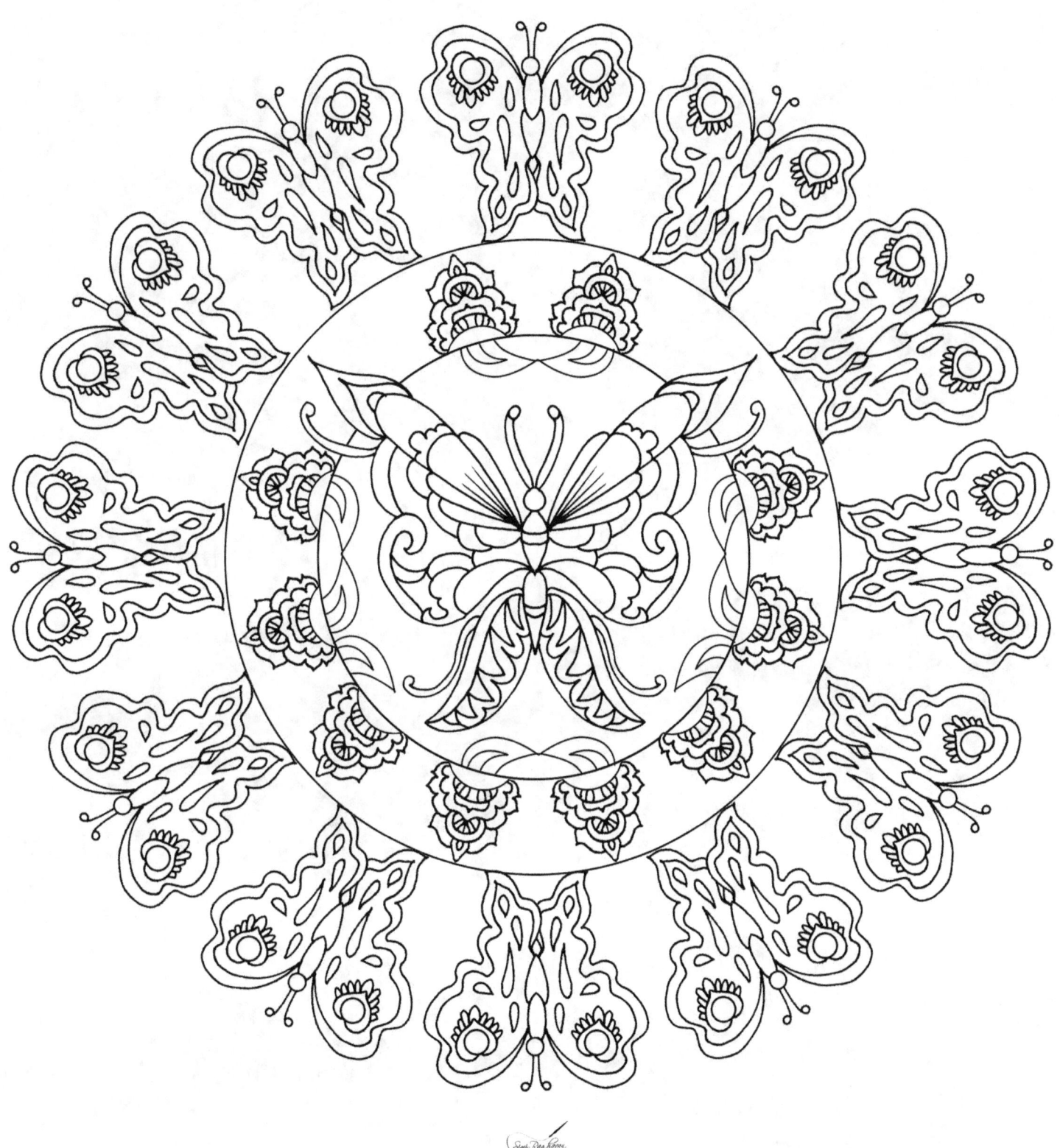

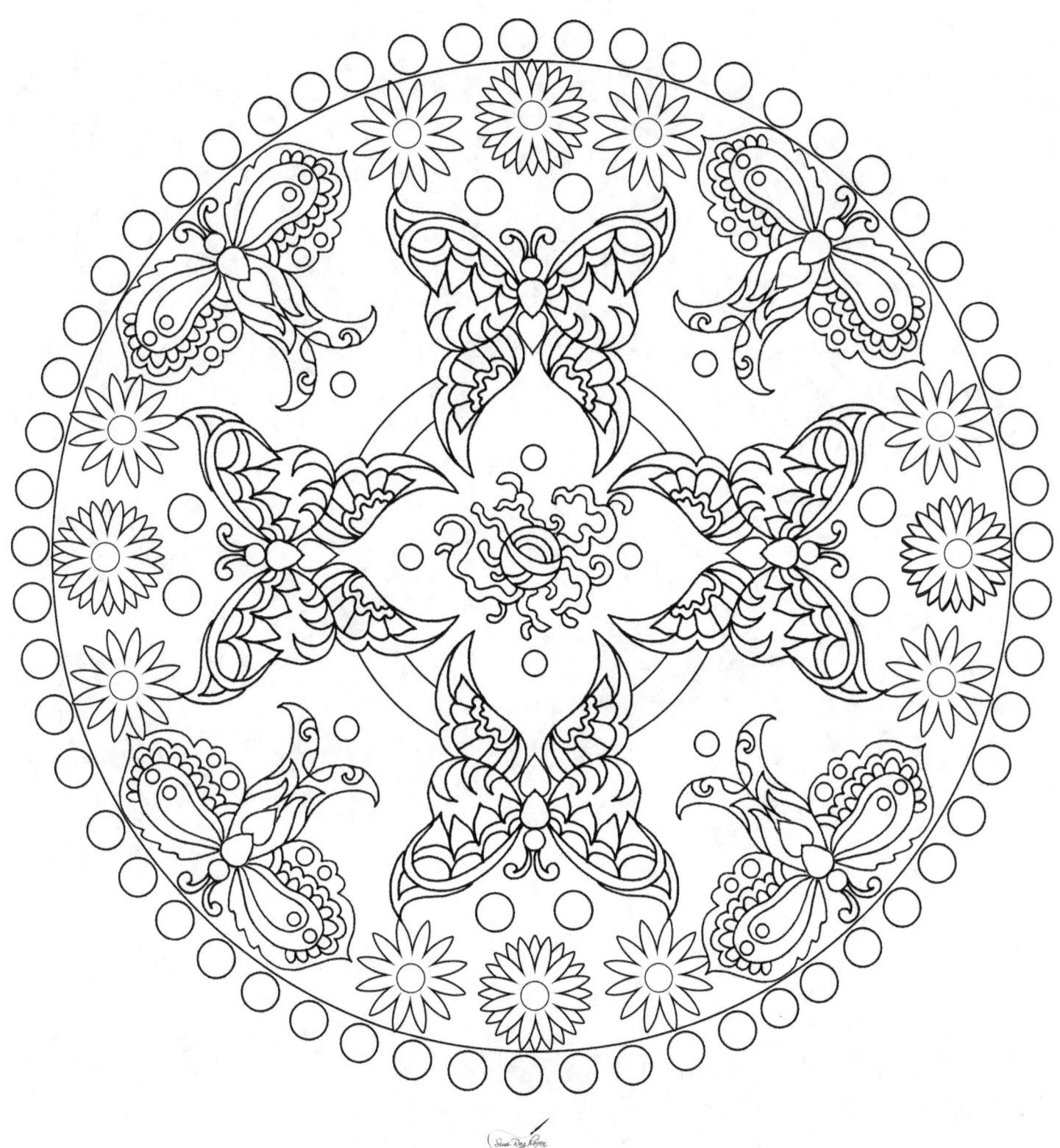

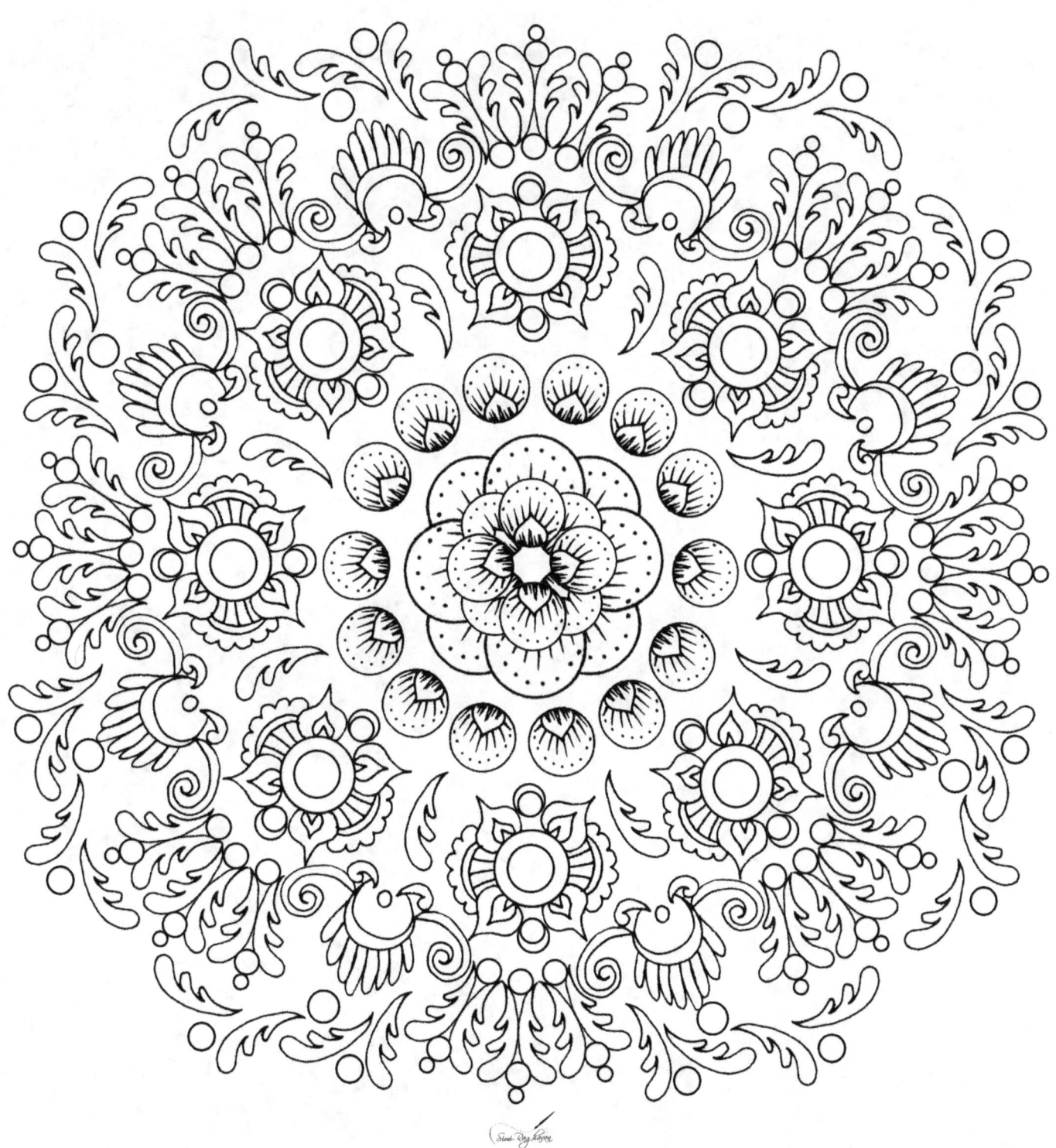